Growing Up

IT'S SCIENCE!

Growing Up

Sally Hewitt

CHILDREN'S PRESS®

A Division of Grolier Publishing

NEW YORK • LONDON • HONG KONG • SYDNEY
DANBURY, CONNECTICUT

Acknowledgments:

Bruce Coleman pp. 7tr (Kim Taylor), 7bl (Jorg and Petra Wegner), 14 (Jane Burton), 16l (M.R. Phicton), 17t (Fritz Prenzel), 19cl (Dr. Eckart Pott), 20l (Jane Burton), 20r (Jane Burton); FLPA pp. 17b (Silvestris), 23t (Brake/Sunset); Sally and Richard Greenhill p. 25t; Robert Harding pp. 10tr; Image Bank p. 24; NHPA pp. 7br (Daniel Heuclin), 22r (Daniel Heuclin), 23b (Nigel J. Dennis); Oxford Scientific Films pp. 15t (Reed Williams), 15b (M.Wilding), 18 (Mike Birkhead), 19tl (Mike Birkhead), 21tl (Breck P. Kent), 21tc (Rudie H. Kruiter), 21tr (Rudie H. Kruiter), 21bl (Rudie H. Kruiter), 21br (John Mitchell), 22bl (Z. Leszcznski); Photofusion pp. 6l (Reen Pilikington), 12 (Clarissa Leahy); Planet Earth Pictures pp. 16r (Frank Krahmer), 19bl (Frank Krahmer), 19tr (Margaret Welby); Stock Market pp. 8tl, 8br, 10l, 10br, 11tl, 11bl, 13. All other photography commissioned by Franklin Watts. With thanks to our model, James Moller.

Series editor: Rachel Cooke
Designer: Mo Choy
Picture research: Alex Young
Photography: Ray Moller unless otherwise acknowledged
Series consultant: Sally Nankivell-Aston

First published in 1998 by Franklin Watts
First American edition 1999 by Children's Press
A Division of Grolier Publishing
90 Sherman Turnpike
Danbury, CT 06816

Visit Children's Press on the Internet at:
http://publishing.grolier.com

Library of Congress Cataloging-in-Publication Data
Hewitt, Sally.
    Growing up / Sally Hewitt. -- 1st American ed.
        p. cm. -- (It's science!)
    Includes index.
    Summary: Considers the ways humans change from birth through adulthood and compares human growth with that of animals.
    ISBN 0-516-21180-3 (lib. bdg.) 0-516-26448-6 (pbk.)
    1. Human growth--Juvenile literature. [1. Growth.] I. Title.
II. Series: Hewitt, Sally. It's science!
QP84.H47 1999
612.6--dc21   97-52163
                                                                    CIP
                                                                    AC

Printed in Malaysia

Contents

Born Today!

This tiny baby has just been born.
When you were a baby like this one, you couldn't do much for yourself.
You needed an **adult** to feed you and keep you safe, clean, and warm.

Young **human** beings have to be looked after by their **parents** for a long time. As we grow up, we learn to do more and more things for ourselves.

THINK ABOUT IT!

Find a picture of yourself as a baby. In what ways do you look different? How much have you grown? What can you do now that you couldn't do then?

Some newly born or newly hatched creatures have to be able to do more for themselves right away than others.

A baby bird must be fed. It has to grow feathers and learn to fly before it can leave the nest.

A baby deer has to walk as soon as it is born so that it can keep up with the **herd**. Its mother still feeds it, though.

A young snake slithers away and survives by itself as soon as it **hatches** from its egg.

Growing Up

Human beings like you take many years to grow up. They need grown-ups to care for them, and give them food and a safe place to live.

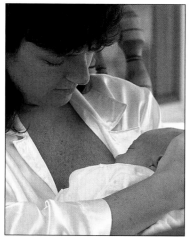

Tina is a new baby. She has no teeth. She needs her mother's milk, which she sucks from her mother's breast. Some babies drink milk from a bottle.

Sarah is thirty years old. She is grown up and has a baby of her own. We call a fully grown person an adult.

John is one year old. He has grown some teeth and can eat all kinds of good food to help him grow strong and healthy. He still likes milk, but now he drinks cow's milk and has it in a cup.

Lee is fifteen years old. He is a **teenager**. He is almost grown up.

Aaron is nine years old. He already has his grown-up teeth. His baby teeth fell out when he was about six years old.

Ali is two years old. He can walk by himself. He has longer legs and more hair than John. What other differences tell you he is older?

TRY IT OUT!

Do you have photographs of yourself on some of your birthdays?
If you have, put them in order of age.
Beside a picture of you on your last birthday, write your height, the size of your feet, how much you weigh, and the date.
Keep a record of you—growing up.

Learning

You are growing all the time. You will stop getting taller when you get older, but you will never stop learning.

Babies begin to learn about the world around them as soon as they are born.

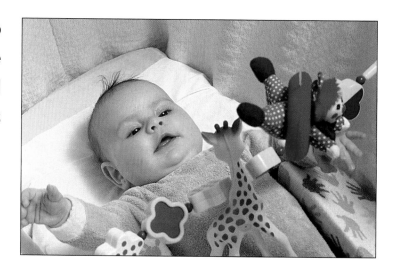

Toddlers learn to walk and talk.

When you go to school, you learn to read and write, to do arithmetic, and to do all kinds of new things.

As you grow older, you learn to do more complicated things. You do not need as much help from other people.

Many teenagers leave home to get a job or go to college.

THINK ABOUT IT!

When you are grown up, you will learn to do a job and earn money for the things you need. What job would you like to do? Why would you like to do it?

11

A New Baby

Did you know you began life as an **egg** about the size of a dot?

A new life begins when a tiny **sperm** from a father joins an egg from a mother. The egg starts to grow inside the mother's womb.

A mother's **womb** is a safe place for a baby to grow until it is ready to be born. You can sometimes feel the baby moving around.

TRY IT OUT!

Find your belly button. It is the place where a tube joined you to your mother when you were growing in her womb. The tube supplied you with food and **oxygen**.

It takes about nine months for the tiny egg to grow into a baby that is ready to leave the safety of its mother's womb and live in the world outside.

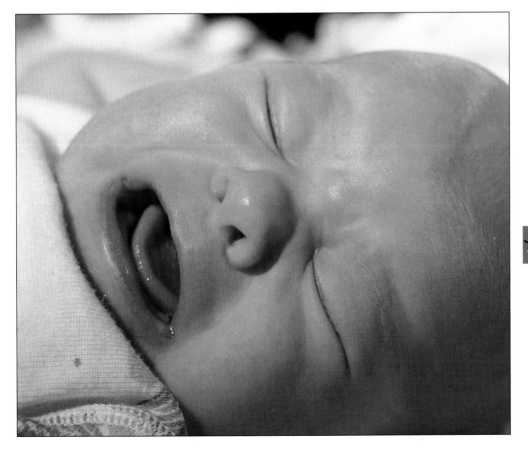

As soon as the baby is born, it takes its first breath of air and often cries very loudly!

LOOK AGAIN

Look again at page 8 to find out what this newborn baby's first meal will be.

Cats and Kittens

A mother cat has about four to six kittens. They grow inside her for eight weeks. They are blind, deaf, and helpless when they are born.

Like the babies of humans and other **mammals**, kittens drink their mother's milk. Their mother feeds them and looks after them until they can go hunting on their own.

💡 **THINK ABOUT IT!**

Pet cats don't look after themselves completely even when they are fully grown. What would you have to do to look after a pet cat?

Have you ever watched kittens play together?
They are learning how to become fierce hunters and to look after themselves. A cat is fully grown and can have kittens of its own before it is a year old.

 **LOOK AGAIN**

Look again at pages 8 and 9. How much more growing and learning does a one-year-old baby still have to do?

15

Pouches

Baby kangaroos have a very unusual place to grow before they are ready to look after themselves—in a pocket!

A tiny baby kangaroo, called a joey, is only 1 in (2.5 cm) long when it is born. It crawls into its mother's pocket which we call a pouch.

It stays in the pouch and sucks milk for about six months, until it is big enough to jump out and look for its own food.

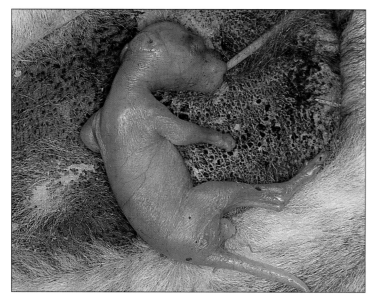

 TRY IT OUT!

Find a ruler and draw a line 1 inch (2.5 cm) long. Now you can see how tiny a joey is when it is born.

Kangaroos, koala bears, and wombats are all a type of animal called a **marsupial**. Marsupials have pouches for their babies to grow in.

Mother koalas carry their babies in their pouches as they climb through the trees.

Wombats are diggers. Can you see why it is a good thing their pouches open backward?

 THINK ABOUT IT!

Human adults pick their babies up in their arms. What other ways have you seen adults carrying their babies around?

Swans and Cygnets

You grew inside your mother's womb. Marsupials grow in their mother's womb and then in her pouch.

All baby birds grow inside eggs laid by their mothers. Eggs are packed full of the food and goodness a chick needs to grow.

This mother swan is sitting on her eggs to keep them warm and safe.

👁 LOOK AGAIN

Look again at page 13 to find how you were fed when you were growing inside your mother.

When there is no more food left in the egg, the new swan is ready to hatch.

It takes a day for the baby swan to tap open the egg and struggle out.

A baby swan is called a **cygnet**. When the cygnet is two days old, it is ready to swim.

A cygnet has feathers different from an adult swan. It won't grow its beautiful white feathers until it is about two years old.

💡 THINK ABOUT IT!

Birds build nests, where they lay their eggs and look after their chicks. The nest keeps them warm and safe. What makes your home a good place for you to grow up in?

Amazing Changes

Amazing changes happen to some creatures as they grow.

These two pictures are of the same type of animal—
an **insect** called a stag beetle.

A stag beetle hatches from its egg as a soft-bodied **larva**.

Later, as it grows, it changes into a fierce-looking adult stag beetle.

 TRY IT OUT!

Make a list of all the things that are different between a stag beetle larva and an adult stag beetle. Now make a list of all the things that are the same.

A butterfly goes through amazing changes as it grows up, too.

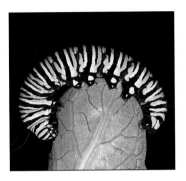

A butterfly lays its eggs on a leaf.

The eggs hatch into caterpillars, which start to munch the leaves.

At the beginning of the summer, the caterpillar hangs on a twig and becomes a **chrysalis**. Inside the chrysalis, amazing changes take place. The caterpillar is turning into a butterfly!

When the butterfly is fully formed, it struggles out of the chrysalis, spreads its wings to dry, and flies away.

Butterflies are the grown-ups. They lay eggs on a leaf and new lives begin.

Reptiles

Most **reptiles** lay eggs. They have different ways of making sure the eggs are kept safe and warm. They grow up in different ways, too.

A female python lays about 100 eggs. She coils her long body around her eggs to make a warm, safe nest.

Snakes grow quickly when they are young. They never stop growing completely until they die.

As snakes get bigger, they grow a new layer of skin and leave the old one behind.

 THINK ABOUT IT!

Very few people live to be a hundred years old. How old is the oldest person you know?

A female crocodile digs a hole in the riverbank for her eggs and covers them with sand.

Crocodile parents guard their eggs to keep them safe from enemies hunting for eggs to eat.

When the baby crocodiles hatch, the mother scrapes away the sand and carries them in her mouth to the river.

Giant Nile crocodiles live for a very long time. It is thought that some of them live to a hundred years old!

Growing Older

Human beings stop growing in height, but we keep changing as we get older.

Emily is three years old, her mother is twenty-nine, her **grandmother** is fifty-five, and her **great-grandmother** is eighty.

Look at the differences between Emily, her mother, her grandmother, and her great-grandmother. How do people change as they get older?

 THINK ABOUT IT!

All living things die—animals, plants, and people. Sometimes people die when they are young because they are ill or have an accident. Most people live a long time and die when they are old.

Sam and his granddad enjoy talking together. Granddad is sixty-five, so he can teach Sam a lot of the things he has learned over many years.

 TRY IT OUT!

Play a matching game. Ask your family, teachers, and friends for photographs of themselves as babies and young children. Pin them up. Can you tell who's who?

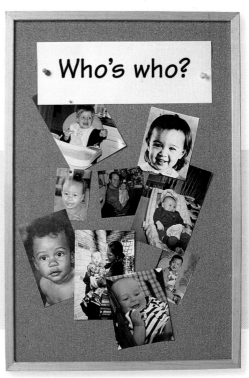

The Cycle of Life

When a new animal is born it becomes part of a **life cycle**. At the end of its life, it dies, but new young animals are born and start new life cycles.

Follow around the circle to find the life cycle of a salmon.

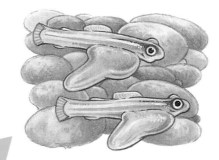

When a baby salmon hatches, it is 1 inch (2.5 cm) long. At first, it feeds off its egg yolk, which it carries with it.

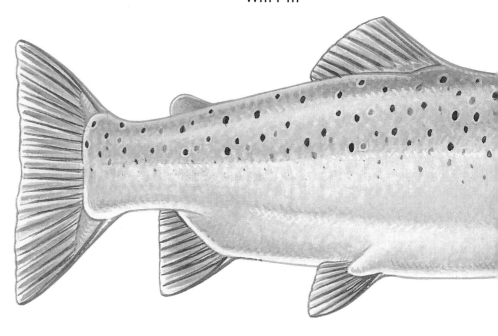

The salmon lays its eggs near the same place it hatched.

The adult salmon finds its way to the river it came from and swims back to it again.

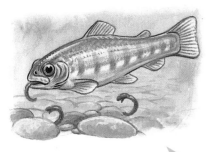

The baby salmon starts to feed on small river creatures. It grows quickly.

After two years, the salmon is about 45 in (18 cm) long. It swims down the river to the ocean.

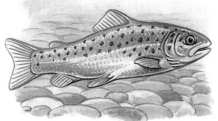

The salmon lives and feeds in the ocean. It grows even more—an adult weighs at least 10 pounds (4.5 kilograms).

TRY IT OUT!

Draw the life cycle of a frog. You need to draw pictures in a circle of frog spawn, tadpoles, a froglet, and an adult frog. Join the pictures with curving arrows. Try drawing a life cycle of another creature that is in this book.

27

Useful Words

Adult A person or animal becomes an adult when they are fully grown.

Chrysalis All butterflies and moths become chrysalises while they are changing from a caterpillar to an adult butterfly.

Cygnet A cygnet is a baby swan.

Egg People and animals start life in an egg. Some animals, including people, keep the egg inside their bodies until the baby inside is ready to be born. Other animals, like birds and most reptiles, lay eggs and the baby animals later hatch from these.

Grandmother Your grandmother is your mother's mother or your father's mother. Your **grandfather** is your mother's father or your father's father.

Great-grandmother Your great-grandmother is the mother of your grandfather or grandmother.

Hatch When a baby animal hatches, it breaks out of the egg and begins its life in the outside world. Baby chicks hatch from birds' eggs.

Herd Grass-eating animals such as deer live and feed together and move around in groups called herds.

Human You are a human. All people —men, women, boys, and girls— belong to a group of animals called humans. Humans are mammals.

Insect Insects are a group of animals with no backbone. Their bodies are divided into three parts and protected by a hard case. They have six legs.

Larva Most insects hatch from an egg as a larva. (The plural of "larva" is "larvae.") Larvae usually look quite different from the adults they grow into. For example, a caterpillar is the larva of a butterfly.

Life cycle Every newborn animal becomes part of a life cycle. It is born, it grows up and has babies of its own (starting new life cycles), and it dies.

Mammals Mammals are a group of animals with backbones. They have some hair or fur. Baby mammals drink milk from their mothers.

Marsupials Marsupials are a group of mammals that have pouches or pockets for their babies to grow in. Kangaroos, koalas, and wombats are all marsupials.

Oxygen Oxygen is a kind of gas that is part of the air we breathe. Our bodies need oxygen to live.

Parent A parent is a mother or father.

Reptiles Reptiles are a group of animals with backbones and scaly, waterproof skin. They breathe air. Some live on land and others in water.

Sperm Sperm is the seed from a father. When a sperm joins an egg from a mother, a new baby begins.

Teenager A teenager is a person aged from thirteen to nineteen—the numbers that end in "teen".

Womb Baby humans and other baby mammals grow inside their mother's womb until they are born.

Index

About This Book

Children are natural scientists. They learn by touching and feeling, noticing, asking questions, and trying things out for themselves. The books in the *It's Science!* series are designed for the way children learn. Familiar objects are used as starting points for further learning. *Growing Up* starts with a new baby and explores human and animal growth.

Each double-page spread introduces a new topic, such as learning. Information is given, questions asked, and activities suggested that encourage children to make discoveries and develop new ideas for themselves. Look for these panels throughout the book:

TRY IT OUT! indicates a simple activity, using safe materials, that proves or explores a point.
THINK ABOUT IT! indicates a question inspired by the information on the page but that points the reader to areas not covered by the book.
LOOK AGAIN introduces a cross-referencing activity that links themes and facts through the book.

Encourage children not to take the familiar world for granted. Point things out, ask questions, and enjoy making scientific discoveries together.